Owls

OWLS

Art, Legend, History

Elena Cenzato and Fabio Santopietro
Series editor: Giorgio Coppin

The Bulfinch Library of Collectibles

A Bulfinch Press Book
Little, Brown and Company
Boston · Toronto · London

First North American Edition

English translation by Graham Fawcett
Edited and adapted by John Gilbert
Series editor: Giorgio Coppin

ISBN 0–8212–1879–4
Library of Congress Catalog Card Number 91–55251
Library of Congress Cataloging-in-Publication information is available.

Bulfinch Press is an imprint and trademark of Little, Brown and Company (Inc.)
Published simultaneously in Canada by Little, Brown & Company (Canada) Limited

PRINTED IN ITALY

CONTENTS

Wiles and charms

Folklore has it that owls are birds of ill omen and that deception is one of their favourite ploys. It is even alleged, in some countries, that these nocturnal birds of prey are possessed by demons. To come across one in the course of a quiet stroll through the forest is therefore as sure a sign of impending disaster as walking under a ladder or seeing a black cat cross your path.

The superstitious hiker is thus at something of a disadvantage. Rather than risk a face-to-face encounter with the fearsome bird, whose hypnotic stare is considered to be capable of rooting him to the spot, unable to escape, he has no choice but to avoid woodland paths altogether.

This view, however, which is by no means universally held, emphasizes the negative aspect of the owl. As counter balance, it has to be said that the bird has been widely admired through the ages by deities, scholars, poets and animal lovers in general, who have accorded it a variety of positive attributes and given it symbolic significance.

In ancient Greece the owl, creature of the night, was

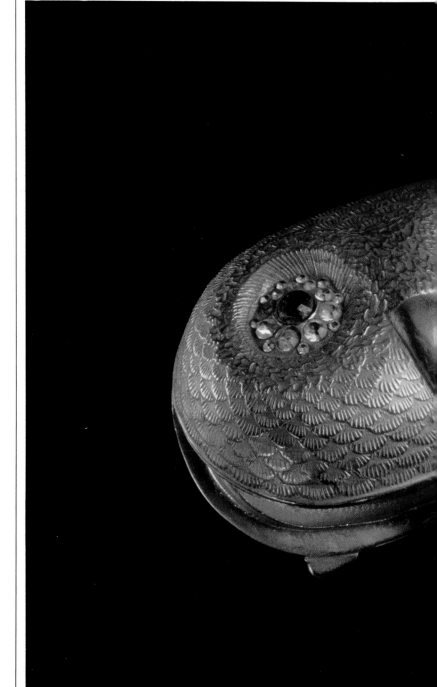

Two wide-eyed modern miniature owls in terracotta. Opposite: two wooden statues made in Thailand in 1928. Depending on the country of origin and time of creation, collectible owls may be regarded as bringers of good fortune or bringers of bad fortune.

associated with the Goddess of Wisdom, Pallas Athene, and images of the bird appeared on early coins of Athens, the city named after her. It was her constant companion and guard, particularly in the hours of darkness, against all manner of stratagems and conspiracies.

Thereafter, the owl, especially in northern Europe and English-speaking countries, came to be seen as a thoughtful, sensible, reliable bird. In many children's books and, more recently, in the film world of Walt Disney, the owl is often depicted in the guise of a stern, bespectacled judge, respected for his sobriety and wisdom.

Yet the symbols themselves have tended to splinter into a labyrinth of different though complementary meanings. Whereas in classical Greece the owl was revered, indeed worshipped, over the centuries its sacred qualities gradually ebbed away. In ancient Rome, and later in medieval

Europe, people went to the opposite extreme and were transfixed by its demonic nature.

In various countries, too, simple words were given different shades of meaning in translation, so that the term "old owl," for example, instead of signifying a wise, experienced person, came to be interpreted, in France and Italy, for example, as a rather distant, sullen, grumpy individual. Owl fans will spring to the defense by pointing out that keeping your distance can itself be a sign of wisdom – you have to stand apart in order to contemplate the world and its ways.

There is thus no incompatibility in these apparently conflicting opinions. Experts in animal behaviour, who have no truck with such notions and warn against the temptation of endowing animals, even those of superior

intelligence, with human emotions, will point out that the solitary habits of owls can be explained simply in terms of genetics, adaptation, distribution and the like. Nevertheless, we cannot resist endowing animals that are familiar to us – our pets, for example – with human attributes. So it might be argued that the very privacy of owls provides them with ample time for reflection and that maybe, as they sit perched

A small family of owls from India, made of very costly materials: coral, copper, cobalt, bronze and turquoise. It is hardly surprising that these nocturnal birds of prey, with their charming, seductive poses, should have been fashioned into works of art.

on a branch at night, watching and waiting, preparatory to the hunt, they are doing more than merely scanning the neighbourhood for moving objects. Humans tend to think that owls, apart from being able to see in the dark, and perhaps as a corollary of this capacity, may also have a gift for comprehending things more deeply than themselves.

Because there are a great number of owl species in continental Europe, the Italians and the French, to give only two examples, have a wide vocabulary to distinguish the various owl types. In Italian, *civetta* is the widely distributed little owl (*Athene noctua*), and both *civetta* and *gufo*, with appropriate suffixes, are used to describe most species of what, in English, are simply "owls." Similarly, French owls are either *hibou* or *chouette*.

In both languages there are thus additional connotations that do not necessarily exist in English-speaking countries. The terms *civetta* and *chouette* have clear associations with the word "coquette," which has a comparable meaning in English; and so there are overtones here of flirtation and seduction that, on the face of it, are quite alien to the bird's more conventional attributes of sobriety and introspection.

In 1494, the Florentine poet Angelo Ambrogini, better known as Poliziano, used the verb *civettare* in the sense of attracting or cajoling someone. Even earlier, the great Italian storyteller Giovanni Boccaccio used the word *zimbello*, signifying both a lure and an owl used as a decoy; and from this comes the Italian verb *zimbellare*, meaning allurement in the widest sense and not merely in a hunting context.

All this adds a little excitement and glamour, perhaps, to the traditional image of the bird; and certainly, the owl's body language can be envisaged, in certain situations, as graceful and alluring. Take, for example, the female great grey owl (*Strix nebulosa*), who, in the presence of her chosen mate, sways her body to and fro, lifting one claw and then the other, this display being accompanied by strange up-and-down head movements and little whimpering cries. This might be interpreted, fancifully, as an exercise in seduction, but both the gestures and the calls, in fact, constitute a perfectly normal form of behaviour among hungry birds of prey; and since it is the food card which the male plays in order to win the favours of the female, she shows her appreciation of his offerings with these typical head and foot movements. Such behaviour is common, moreover, among other owl species.

Owls, in addition, exhibit another unusual and rather disconcerting habit, that of twisting their neck and head back to front. This again has nothing to do with playing games, let alone enticing the opposite sex, but is a wholly natural phenomenon, related to its powers of eyesight.

Above: a piece of Mexican pottery in the shape of an owl. The highly stylized design is typical of Latin American countries. Opposite: three owls sculpted in soapstone, an example of the craftsmanship of India.

Ornithologists tell us that owls are equipped with a tubular eye with a highly developed crystalline lens, rather like a miniature telescope. Moreover, the owl's retina incorporates a series of rods – the type of photoreceptor that is most sensitive to light – and is up to one hundred times superior, in this respect, to the human retina.

The eyes of the owl are fixed and it has binocular vision like our own, but whereas our normal field of vision is about 180°, of which some 140° are covered by binocular vision, the comparable figures for an owl are about 110° and 70° respectively.

Despite its very keen nocturnal vision, the bird's ability to judge distances and distinguish shapes is therfore not as good as our own, but to compensate for these limitations, the neck and head are astonishingly flexible. So if you should happen to come across an owl with its body facing one

This merry-go-round from Italy was carved out of wood. The owl sitting on the platform looks as if it is being used as a decoy, except that there are butterflies, not birds, flying around its head. Hunters in Italy and elsewhere still use owls to catch smaller birds even though there are laws prohibiting it.

direction and its head another, there is absolutely no cause for alarm; the raptor is simply trying to pinpoint an object or line it up better for an attack.

These conspicuous distortions of the head led the ancient Romans to believe that it was the simplest trick in the world to catch an owl. All you had to do was locate your owl sitting on its branch, then walk around the tree three times in the expectation that the head would follow you about until the neck was so twisted that the poor creature just toppled down dead.

As evidence that the owl is not given to sexual enticement or promiscuous behaviour, it should be emphasized that the birds are absolutely monogamous; once they have mated, they maintain this affectionate, harmonious relationship for the rest of their lives. This is not all that common in the bird world – or, for that matter, among mammals either – where multiple mating with different partners tends to be habitual.

It may be that the association of owlishness with feminine wiles harks back to various barbaric hunting practices, dating back at least to the Middle Ages, and some of which, regrettably, persist to this day. Owls appear to have the ability of attracting game birds merely by sitting stock-still on their roosts. The custom arose therefore, for owls to be used as decoys, either tethered or fitted up with netting. Enormous numbers of crows, magpies, jackdaws and even skylarks were shot in Europe, using owls as lures, and the same practice, although illegal elsewhere, is still common in parts of northern Italy where little owls are captured, harnessed and suitably positioned as a decoy for songbirds that are shot for sport.

Although hunters involved in this type of activity may well have believed that owls customarily attracted their prey

by staring steadily at them and virtually hypnotizing them, the traditional use of an owl as a decoy perhaps has a far simpler and mundane explanation. Small birds are probably driven to attack a fettered owl because the raptor is their common enemy. It is a fact that even in the wild, and given complete freedom, owls and other raptors often have to withstand mass assaults, known as mobbing, from smaller birds that recognize them instinctively as their natural foes.

It is hard to understand why owls should have gained a reputation for deceit and trickery, but there are two celebrated legends in which owls play a prominent role in events that involve illicit love and consequent punishment. One of the tales is from Greece, the other from Wales, and both culminate in the guilty women being transformed into owls.

The first of these tales, mentioned by Ovid and told at greater length by Hyginus the Astronomer, a second-century Roman who also wrote fables, concerns Nyctimene, the daughter of King Nycteus. Unfortunately, Nyctimene was desperately in love with her father. Unable to reveal her secret to anyone, she withdrew into solitude and silence, inexplicably refusing the many suitors who came to offer marriage.

This stubborn behaviour aroused the suspicions of her shrewd old nurse, whose incessant questioning finally broke down the girl's defenses and elicited from her the confession of incestuous passion. All attempts to dissuade her were in vain, and when Nyctimene threatened to commit suicide, the nurse reluctantly agreed to arrange a clandestine meeting, bringing the princess in disguise to the king. That night, and for several nights following, the couple made love, until curiosity so overcame Nycteus that he held a lamp close to the mysterious girl's face.

The king's horror, when he discovered her true identity, was indescribable. His daughter, torn by remorse, fled the kingdom. In fact, she literally flew away, for Athene providentially came to her rescue and saved her from certain death by changing her into an owl.

An obvious case of deception, admittedly, but it is hard to see why the owl, in particular, had to answer for the consequences. After all, two of the guilty people, the king and the nurse, continued to go about their everyday affairs, presumably suffering from no more than conscience. Justice would surely have dictated the same fate for them. The transformation of Nyctimene into an owl was evidently intended as a punishment for something much more serious

than simple flirtation and seduction, namely her encouragement of incest and shameful act of illicit love.

In another tale of guilty passion, which involved attempted murder if not incest, punishment of a similar nature was meted out to a heroine of Celtic legend. It is told in the collection of medieval tales of chivalry known as the *Mabinogion*, dating from the eleventh to the thirteenth centuries, and it concerns a lady named Blodeuwedd. Her fate was decided, as indeed her very origins had been, by the celebrated Welsh king Math fab Mathonwy, renowned for his extraordinary magical powers. Math had already punished two of his nephews, found guilty of treason, by turning them first into fawns, then pigs, and finally wolves. When they had learned their lesson, he mercifully restored them to human form, to resume their lives as warriors.

In yet another demonstration of his supernatural gifts, King Math conjured Blodeuwedd out of thin air by a magic spell. Happily married, but left alone too frequently in the castle by her husband Lleu, she fell hopelessly in love one day with a handsome young warrior who happened to ride past. They became lovers and decided to get rid of the unsuspecting husband. The only problem was that Lleu was virtually immortal. Nevertheless, he had an Achilles heel, determined by a strange combination of circumstances: he was likely to die only if he happened to be on the shore of a river at sunset taking a bath in a bathing hut made of straw, while a goat was bleating in the vicinity.

This was an improbable set of simultaneous events, hardly encouraging for the conspirators, but Blodeuwedd and her lover were a ruthless and determined pair. The lady managed to persuade her husband, partly as a dare, partly as a joke, to tempt the hand of fate. Lleu, in all innocence, obediently went off to the river to bathe in the hut, in

A colourful oven-glove in the shape of an owl, from China. The ancient Chinese considered the bird to represent an excess of yang, the active and assertive male principle, over yin. The bird was reputed to cause droughts and to confer a violent nature to children born on the "day of the owl."

exactly the circumstances foretold, and was immediately struck down. Instead of dying, however, he was miraculously changed into a mighty eagle; and so he remained until, thanks to the skills of King Math, the lovers' act of deception was uncovered. Soon afterwards, an owl was seen gliding across the Welsh skies. It was Blodeuwedd.

The allegedly seductive character of the owl is a theme that recurs in literature and legend and was supposedly verified by observation of the animal's behaviour, though these observations are of an all too fanciful nature. Thus Claudius Aelianus, a Roman writer who lived from

The stable relationship of pairs of owls is well exemplified in this small bronze sculpture from the foundry school of Brescia, in northern Italy: the single block of metal is proof against human snares. Opposite: the plastic comb with glass eyes is another amusing piece from the Fornasetti collection.

A.D. 170 to 230, wrote a work entitled *De natura animalium*, a mishmash of fact and fiction concerning the fauna of his day. Aelianus maintained that the owl was akin to a witch or sorceress, capable of attracting other birds by mysterious stratagems, based on the "scientific" assumption that, like some quick-change artist, it could adopt any number of different appearances, even changing its facial features according to the prey it happened to be tracking. The victim, accordingly, would be hypnotized by the predator's metamorphosis and surrender meekly to its clutches.

Aelianus, in fact, was merely following a firmly established tradition that dated back to the myths of Greece. For example, the beautiful nymph Calypso, daughter of Atlas, sole inhabitant of the island of Ogygia, lived in a cave where her companions were falcons, choughs and owls. The owl, indeed, was her emblem. No surprise, therefore, that Calypso should have used all her seductive wiles to lure the shipwrecked Greek hero, Ulysses, into a life devoted wholly to idle comforts, under the everlasting protection of the gods. Ulysses, of course, refused to yield to the nymph's

*An owl made of iron wire and variously tinted glass, from Uruguay. Although this is apparently an eagle-owl (*Bubo bubo*), he looks more like a court jester than a fearsome bird of prey.*

charms, preferring to continue his journey back to his homeland, where his steadfast wife, Penelope, awaited him.

Yet we have to look back even further than the days of ancient Greece and Rome, when such legends were formulated, for the origins of these beliefs. Owls, which make up the order Strigiformes, are many millions of years old. It may be surmised that to the early hominids the ghostly forms and weird, hooting cries of these nocturnal hunting birds inspired conflicting emotions, ranging from terror to reverence, and that superstition, reinforced by oral tradition, gradually endowed them with symbolic values. Hence they came to be associated with powers both of good and evil, the sacred juxtaposed with the profane.

Mysterious hunters of the night

Long before human beings appeared on Earth – and paleontologists, basing their theories on discoveries of fossil remains, are still debating exactly when this happened – the ancestors of present-day owls were already flitting silently through the night on their hunting missions. So it may be that in some corner of its biological memory, the owl retains images of dinosaurs, huge reptile-like birds, enormous fish and early mammals, all of which were to vanish completely, apart from a few represented primitive forms of species that survive to this day.

Birds, strange as it may seem, are more closely related to reptiles than to any other vertebrate group. The first forms, judging from fossils, evolved from small dinosaurs about 190 million years ago. But the owls developed somewhat later, about 135 million years ago, according to the oldest fossils so far discovered, in which case they would only have witnessed the death throes of the dinosaurs – and the exact manner in which these enormous creatures became extinct is yet another matter of scientific speculation.

In an environment where animals, whether on the ground, in the sea or in the air, tended to fall into the category either of predator or prey, the owls established themselves as specialized hunters, creatures essentially of darkness. Then, as today, they feared few enemies. High in the trees, they could look down indifferently on the huge, powerful mammals that reigned supreme below – creatures that, in any event, were also doomed to extinction. And, after all, that advanced two-legged animal, known as man, was a much later arrival.

Theories as to how hominids – the ancestors of modern humans – evolved continue to preoccupy paleontologists

An Italian brick-fired lantern, which can look very impressive when hung on a tree with the flickering flame visible through the owl's eyes. Opposite: the austerity of the eagle-owl is finely portrayed in this valuable crystal piece.

and anthropologists, and estimates of when and where they first appeared fluctuate almost from year to year, according to the latest fossil discoveries. But this is not the place to discuss the route by which *Homo sapiens* finally arrived on this planet. Regardless of the relationship of man and ape, humans are distinguished from other animals by their permanently upright stance and the complexity of their brain. Gradually they brought their special skills and intelligence to bear on the world around them, influencing their environment, for better or worse; and in their struggle for survival, aided by sophisticated tools and deadly weapons, they formed relationships with other animals, either hunting them for food or domesticating them for work and companionship.

The owl never fit into this simple pattern of roles. Indeed, it is probable that man, from the start, was fascinated and somewhat perplexed by this strangely impassive,

A Mexican owl in coloured plaster for use as a wall decoration: a palpably less spine-chilling practice than hanging a real flesh-and-blood owl carcass on the front door of the house to avert the evil eye. Following double page: two owls from the Trentino-Alto Adige region of northern Italy, small-scale sculptures made from various kinds of dried seed heads and fruits.

unusual-looking bird, and, moreover, was somewhat uneasy in its presence. There may have been a hint of envy, too, for it was evident that the owl, in several respects, had the advantage of man. Not only could it see much better in darkness and half-light than he could, but it gave the impression, with its much longer experience and impassive aspect, of being infinitely wise.

The first recorded contact between humans and owls occurred during the Paleolithic or Old Stone Age, at the time when the Cro-Magnon people, our direct ancestors, lived in Europe. These hunter-gatherers made stone tools and weapons, hunted woolly mammoths and bison, and left astonishing pictorial records of their lives and surroundings on the walls of caves.

At the Trois-Frères cave, in the Pyrenees, the Abbé Breuil discovered one painting that depicted a curious figure of a man with antlers. Experts in prehistoric art called it "The Sorcerer." The subject's erect posture and genitals identify it as a human, even though the remainder of the body was a kind of animal collage, including the head of a crow, the face of an owl, the ears of a wolf and the beard of a chamois.

"The Sorcerer" is very probably a sacred individual or shaman, and the position of the limbs suggests he is dancing, possibly enacting a form of ritual calculated to bring about success in the hunt. In similar cave paintings, the animals depicted are often those that would have been regularly hunted for food and other basic needs, such as the mammoth, the rhinoceros, the bison and the bear. The animals portrayed in this one, however, do not fall obviously into that category and may, therefore, have

A collage by Giannantonio Ossani entitled "Owl" (1987). Opposite: from Japan, an ivory button in the shape of an owl with eyes out on stalks. It was originally worn to ward off the evil eye, which, so the legend goes, strikes if you see an owl.

symbolic as well as magical significance. By portraying the face of the owl, the unknown artist might not only be endeavouring to win the bird's favour but also ensuring that the hunter be endowed with the owl's keen, penetrating eyesight, especially at night.

The shaman, half-priest, half-doctor, traditionally played a significant role in propitiatory rites for the capture of wild animals. The creatures inspired mingled feelings of fear and respect in those who hunted them. Whether or not such an animal turned out to be hostile or friendly depended on how effective these rituals were. In some cases, an animal took on totemic significance, so that an individual's life became closely linked with that creature, to the point of actually assuming its natural characteristics and attributes.

Sir James Frazer, the British anthropologist, author of *The Golden Bough*, gives examples of totemism that have

persisted in primitive communities until modern times. The Wotjobaluk tribe of southeastern Australia, held the firm belief that the lives of its women were influenced by Yàrtatgurk, the owl, and those of men by the bat. So much so, says Frazer, that "if my brother John's life is in a bat, then, on the one hand, the bat is my brother as well as John . . . and if my sister Mary's life is in an owl, then the owl is my sister and Mary is an owl." This conviction was so deeply rooted that if a man of the tribe was unfortunate enough to kill an owl by mistake, all the women would turn on him, and bitter conflict would break out between the sexes (". . . at times the women gave the men a severe drubbing with their yamsticks"), with unpredictable consequences.

In ancient Greece, owls were familiar and auspicious birds. One Greek myth tells of Ascalaphus, the young son of Acheron and Night. At the time the Titans were waging war against Zeus, Acheron had been flung into Hades and had lived there ever since. This miserable existence evidently did not prevent him fathering a child. Ascalaphus, when he grew up, distinguished himself by becoming an informer.

Persephone, the daughter of Zeus and Demeter, had been imprisoned by Pluto, god of Hades, who had eventually agreed to her returning to the upper world provided she did not eat anything on her journey. Ascalaphus revealed to Zeus that Persephone had, in fact, disobeyed this injunction by eating seven seeds of a pomegranate. Zeus himself did not seem particularly shocked either by the revelation or the deed, but Demeter, outraged, took revenge on her daughter's betrayor by splashing Ascalaphus' face with water from the river Phlegethon, thus turning him into an owl.

Demeter was mistaken, however, in thinking that

An objet trouvé *representing an owl. It is the work of Carlo Mo, dating from 1985. The base is in wood, while the bird's body is made from an ordinary metal corkscrew and the head from a round piece of metal with shaped eyes.*

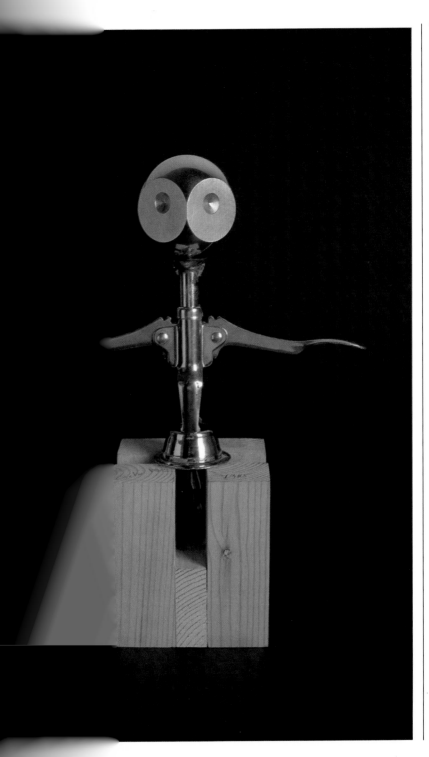

Above: a silver bracelet in the form of an eagle-owl, made in Italy. Opposite: a bottle opener in enamelled metal from Greece, showing the bird associated with Athene, goddess of fertility and wisdom.

Ascalaphus would be seriously harmed by her transformation. On the contrary, it led directly to his enjoying the best of fortune. The goddess Athene extended him her protection as a faithful ally, capable of seeing everything that went on by night. Thereafter, owls of all kinds were marshalled into her service, keeping their eyes and ears open for any conspiracies hatched against her under cover of nightfall.

In Apuleius' *Golden Ass*, there is a metamorphosis of a rather different nature. Lucius, the hero, embarks on a passionate love affair with a slave girl, Fotis, his real aim being to persuade her to give away the magic secrets of her mistress, Pamphile, who is a witch. Lucius, however, pays dearly for dabbling in the black arts.

Fotis conducts him to Pamphile's room, where he

watches her transform herself into an owl. Before his eyes,

Pamphile's limbs are gradually covered with feathers, her nose grows horny and beaked, her nails turn into talons. Then, after a few experimental hops, she glides away, hooting, over the rooftops.

Lucius begs Fotis to give him access to the magic potion so that he can reproduce this feat. He longs to be turned into an owl, the bird of wisdom, despite the risk he runs of being caught and nailed with open wings to a doorpost (evidence that even in Greece, where the owl was revered, there was a streak of cruelty underneath), but asks Fotis to make sure there is another magic potion on hand to turn himself back into a handsome young man. Unfortunately, things go badly wrong. After he smears himself with Pamphile's ointment, he finds, to his horror, that his hair is getting coarse, his skin hardening into hide, his hands becoming hooves, and that he is growing a long tail. In short, he has become an ass.

There are numerous references to owls, too, in Christian lore. A tale, for example, in the *Bestiary of Christ*, from Charbonneau-Lassay, relates how in France the presence of an owl was welcome and comforting to travellers at night. The owls not only kept them company, communicating with hoots and whistles, but also kept an eye out for obstacles on the path. Legend has it in southern France and

Spain that owls achieve such powerful strength of vision by refuelling their eyes from altar lamps, finding their way at night into churches for this very purpose. This explains why, in the neighbourhood of Nice, they were nicknamed "sussa lampea," or "lamp-suckers."

Beliefs of this kind have clearly persisted through the centuries. Ishmael Moya, the Argentinian author of a curious book on American superstitions, recalls having met a remarkable woman healer who claimed to be able to "see" illnesses and then cure them by the simple expedient of looking into the eyes of her stuffed owl.

Owls, presumably in their role as clairvoyants, also feature in heraldry. The Breton coat of arms, for instance, bears the figure of a golden owl on a green background, representing a bird that can see things no matter how occult they may be, and by virtue of this exceptional power, is accounted wise.

Thus, though a creature of darkness and the night, through its acute eyesight and "wise" aspect, the owl also became associated with vision, wisdom and clairvoyance. This progression of associations from darkness to light is responsible for the owl being credited with an assortment of powers, whether for good or ill, which came to acquire symbolic significance. And it is the nature of the owl's solitary surroundings, as well as its almost exclusively nocturnal habits, that has given rise to such a wealth of superstitious beliefs in all parts of the world where the bird is normally found.

Papier-mâché owl made in Mexico. The owl is traditionally an emblem of soothsayers, and among the Aztecs it was dubbed "caretaker of the dark house of the earth." The large eye dominating the lower half of the figurine may be meant to reinforce this idea.

A hermit's life: solitude and wisdom

Observations in the field suggest that owls spend most of their lives on their own. Only on rare occasions and in specific circumstances do they abandon their solitary habits and come together briefly to make social contact with one another.

For the majority of species, territory is of vital importance, for within this circumscribed area the bird will carry out all its essential activities, hunting, feeding, nesting, roosting, breeding and raising young. Once an owl has laid claim to a patch – and it may be quite a small one – it will noisily announce its presence, defend it against rivals and enemies, and sometimes continue to occupy it year after year.

As a rule, the owl will not take the trouble to construct a nest of its own but will scour around looking for a ready-made home, perhaps a nest abandoned by another species, a hollow in a tree, a depression on the ground, a wall cavity of a ruined building, a barn roof or even a church belfry. Indeed, the bird is a great opportunist, and provided there

*A modern metal money box. The Greeks
also saw the owl as a symbol of wealth and
thriftiness. Opposite: an owl carved out of
marble by Mario Molteni in 1988.*

are plenty of rodents in the neighbourhood, is not too
particular as to a nesting site. Some species may be induced
to occupy a nest box, in which case they will become
accustomed to humans in the vicinity. As a rule, however,
fairly secluded places are preferred, including cemeteries.

The name of the owl order, Strigiformes, and the generic
name *Strix* to describe a large number of species, suggests an
undeservedly sinister reputation, for *strix*, in Latin, is a
witch, reflected also in the Italian word for witch, *strega*.
The scientific name of the tawny owl, for example, is *Strix
aluco*, and the great grey owl, the Ural owl and the barred
owl are other species which belong to this genus, although
there is no reason to believe that these are more likely to be
associated with sorcery than any of the others. Yet the
conviction that owls are inseparably linked with witchcraft
is widespread throughout Europe and also in Asia and

Africa. The belief is reinforced by their natural habits. Thus the fact that owls sometimes choose a cemetery for roosting has led to their being associated with demons and evil spirits. A chance meeting in such a place may therefore dictate immediate and drastic countermeasures such as exorcism. In some parts of South America, it is considered essential to get out of the graveyard as soon as possible, without lowering one's gaze and repeating the words, "I believe in God and not in you." This has the effect of avoiding the curse and repelling the demon that appears in the guise of an owl.

Superstitions of this nature go back many centuries. The people of Pre-Columbian Latin America were alarmed and terrified by the characteristic hooting cry of the bird, wavering in pitch, as it echoed through the impenetrable darkness, and they reacted in a variety of bizarre ways. For instance, whenever the mournful cry of an owl was heard, the Araucanians proceeded to make as much noise as possible to frighten off the evil spirits, banging objects against the walls of their huts and shouting at the top of their voices. And since owls were found in great numbers in the neighbourhood, nights literally became nightmares.

Don José, a monk who visited these parts in the course of his missionary travels in the sixteenth century, reported that these were the noisiest people he had ever come across.

It is interesting to note that in the Bible, owls are classified among the many animals traditionally regarded as unclean. Yet again, the origin of such a belief is rooted in misunderstanding. The owl was deemed inedible because it hunted and fed on carrion and was despised because it preferred to live in what the Book of Leviticus terms "barren" places. The prophet Isaiah declares that after the destruction of the corrupt city of Babylon, only the owls will be left to inhabit the devastated areas, and satyrs will dance in the ruins.

In ancient Rome, the owl fared little better, and few people had a good word for it. Pliny, for example, stressed the fact that the owl inhabited not only the deserts and similar unpopulated places but also those that were extremely difficult to reach – another reference to its preference for quiet and seclusion. The poet Ovid obviously thought that the owl's tendency to inhabit inhospitable sites was the direct punishment for wrong doing, when he wrote that they ". . . avoid the eyes of men and the light, and hide their shame in darkness, and are driven from the sky by all the other birds."

Automatically, therefore, the bird was taken for a demon, inspiring fear that was little short of obsessive. In the event of an owl perching on or near the Capitol, the Romans immediately embarked on an elaborate ritual of purificatory washing and cleansing in order to avoid possible owl-related disasters.

Here and in other societies, the unfortunate bird was thus

Opposite: a valuable sculpture in semi-precious stone from India. Following double page: an Art Nouveau photograph holder in wood and tin. There are two owls involved here, one quite clearly visible between the pair of photographs, the other merely hinted at by the decoration of the frame and by the picture holes themselves, which are its eyes.

transformed into something of a social outcast for no better reason than the fact that it was a silent, nocturnal predator. As an illustration of the punishment that awaits the miserly, and hence the godless, there is a famous story, extant in two versions, concerning a baker's daughter from the city of Gloucester in England, who steals the loaf that her pious mother has baked for Jesus Christ himself. Because of this graceless display of greed, the girl is at once turned into an owl.

In the second, slightly different version of the tale, the daughter cuts the bread into two, reckoning that the entire

loaf is too much for Jesus to eat. But, after she has done this, the bread grows and grows until it is an enormous loaf. Confronted by this miracle, the girl is astounded and starts to yell and screech. At this point, unsurprisingly, she develops the wings and hooked beak of an owl.

A very old Spanish tale, of rather a melancholy strain, endeavours to explain this social discrimination against owls. Once upon a time, the owl was blessed with the most beautiful song of all the birds, but because it had the singular misfortune to be a witness of Christ's crucifixion, it was fated from that day onward to shun the daylight evermore

– and hence to be a social outcast. So scarred was the poor bird by the spectacle that instead of its lovely, warbling song, all that now issued from its throat was a pitiful, monotonous *cruz, cruz,* which in Spanish is the word for the Cross.

A similar theme is echoed in a story from central Europe that tells of a time when all the birds gathered to elect their own king. They decided that the most deserving claimant to the throne should be the bird that proved its prowess by flying to a greater height than any other. The eagle, as might have been predicted, soared highest; convinced of victory, it

An owl on its perch is the design on the label of this old matchbox from Japan. Opposite: a pair of gilt owls from Thailand, made from wood and pitch.

felt that it was safe to take a rest and proceeded to glide lazily in circles. However, it had not reckoned with the resourcefulness of the tiny wren, which had hidden away by perching in the eagle's tail feathers. At this point, it took off, fluttered a few feet into the air above the eagle's head, and so tricked its rival into defeat.

The assembled parliament of birds refused to accept this deceitful result of the contest and put the wren into prison, where it was guarded by that incomparable sentinel, the owl. Untrue to form, however, instead of keeping close, continuous watch on its prisoner, the owl closed its eyes for forty winks, thus giving the wren an unexpected opportunity to escape. Out of shame, the owl henceforth never had the courage to show its face in the light of day.

Although the owl is disgraced in the end, it does not emerge from the proceedings with its reputation in tatters;

in fact, it retains a modicum of dignity. But in another version of the same tale, featuring the same characters, the owl suffers a worse fate. The wren, in this instance, has lost all its feathers and is not so much the culprit as the victim. The other birds unanimously display a generous spirit and offer to provide the destitute wren with some of their own feathers. Only the owl refuses point-blank to part with any, arguing that with winter coming, and because it fears the cold, it cannot spare them. The birds are affronted and their king decides to punish the owl's meanness by condemning it to a friendless, nocturnal existence in lonely places; and should it dare to show its face during the day, it is threatened with pursuit and merciless persecution by all the other birds. This would explain not only why the owl customarily hunts at night but also why, when it does modify its predatory habits by venturing into the open by day, it is frequently mobbed by hosts of smaller birds.

Certain legends of the Native Americans show the owl in a rather more sympathetic guise. At one time, during the golden age, humans and animals lived in a state of perfect harmony and concord. But this age passed, disputes began to arise between the two kingdoms, and the Great Spirit, weary of the dissension and strife that was tearing the world apart, set out across the sea, vowing never to return until all these bitter disagreements had been resolved. This was why the owl habitually uttered its nightly cry of *chu, chu, chu,* which to the acute ear of the Native American signified, "Oh, I am sad!"

The emphasis is somewhat different. Whereas the image of the owl has previously been decidedly negative, there is a hint of recognition that the poor bird may have some good points as well. It is described as being unique, even supernatural, a bearer of the spirit and guardian of the soul.

This owl from Greece, a magnificent example of enamelled earthenware, is the essence of wisdom in solitude. Ever since classical times, and especially in Greek culture, owls have been considered the wisest of birds.

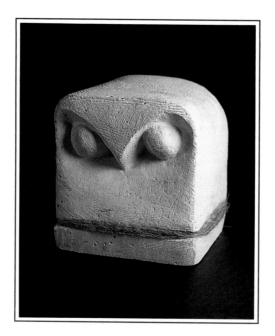

So a chink of light in the darkness may be discerned here.

By and large, though, in the New World as in the Old, there is a deep-rooted inclination to be suspicious of owls and to slander them. Should you happen to hear the owl calling in a wood, an imitation of the cry may serve to ward off the evil eye; but if your version of the call is inaccurate, this counter spell has no effect and the owl's hooting remains a message of ill-omen.

In Alabama, prompt action of a different kind helps to avert trouble. The moment the owl stops hooting, you simply remove one of your shoes and hurl it in that direction. Should the positions be reversed, and the owl is heard calling from indoors and you are outside, the shoe should be thrown across the threshhold. As a variation of this somewhat impetuous remedy, you may take off any convenient article of clothing and put it on again inside-out, provided the owl has already flown away.

A more drastic and certainly crueller solution, also from North America, requires you to have an open fire blazing in the grate and a red-hot poker ready to hand. It presupposes,

Below: another owl from Thailand, which, here, is featured in a small and very colourful container made of enamel on copper. Opposite: an Italian owl in cement and twine (1978), made by Giovanni Canu.

too, that the owl is sitting close by waiting to have its claws scorched. Not surprisingly, this will quieten its hooting and cause it to concentrate on the more urgent matter of seeking cool water to ease the burning.

Superstitious beliefs die hard and all too often give rise to behaviour quite disproportionate to the alleged offense. In an attempt to clear the owl's name and guard against cruel practices that dated back to olden times, the Italian writer Giuseppe Gené, in the nineteenth century, published a book entitled *Dei pregiudizi intorno agli animali* (Of Popular Prejudices Relating to Animals). Gené attacked, among

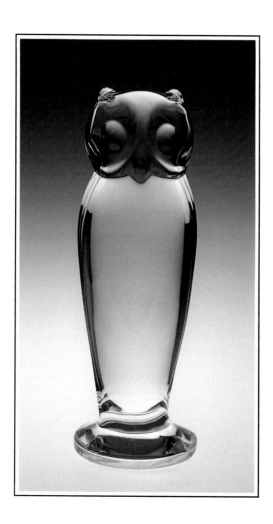

*An accurate modern reproduction of a typical
classical Greek decorative ornament.
Opposite: a stylized eagle-owl in blown
glass, made in Venice in the 1950s.*

other things, the barbaric custom common almost
everywhere in Europe of nailing the owl's carcass to the
door of the house, stemming from the erroneous belief that
the raptor killed and ate farmyard animals or domestic birds
such as doves. The truth is, of course, that the owl preys
almost exclusively on vermin and thus is an ally to the
farmer, a fact which Gené recognized in pointing out that
the bird is useful rather than harmful and as good as, if not
better than, a cat in catching mice.

By way of exploding the myth that holds the owl is a
messenger of death because it occasionally perches on the
roof of a home where a person is dying, Gené shrewdly and
pragmatically observed that an owl is just as likely to settle
and call on the eaves of a house in which the occupants all
enjoy the best of health. Logically, therefore, it could
equally be seen as an augury of *good* fortune.

All the popular beliefs and superstitions about owls,
including the assumptions that they bring bad luck, rest on
the shakiest of foundations, although logical explanations
are not necessarily proof against firmly held prejudices. Nor

can they all be put to the test as easily as the theory of the aforementioned Aelianus who alluded to the owl's sensitivity to changes in the weather.

Aelianus was convinced that if an owl cried on a fine day, a heavy shower was in the offing, and that a similar cry on a rainy day meant that the weather was about to clear up. This is hardly a difficult forecast for anyone to make, particularly in a changeable climate, since it is inevitable that, sooner or later, rain will be followed by sunshine, and vice versa. Any reasonable person will conclude that owls are far from being clairvoyants in this literal sense.

Even though weather forecasting may be rather far-fetched, there is no denying that the mere outward appearance of the owl does suggest something out of the ordinary. Its solemn gaze and sedate, calm composure undoubtedly convey an air of self-reliance and inner depth. Moreover, the oval head, flattened in front by the so-called facial disc, the large eyes and the tufts of feathers surrounding the ears combine to reinforce that aura of gravity and concentration that seems to endow them with something akin to a human semblance.

As likely as not, the owl is listening rather than thinking. Indeed, it is possible to come within a few feet of a great grey owl without disturbing it, so rapt is the bird's concentration as it employs its finely tuned sense of hearing to detect certain sounds that are absolutely inaudible to humans. Whether this is a sign of wisdom is a moot point. Some people who have observed the rigid posture and facial expression of an owl during daylight hours suggest that it simply looks dazed and absent.

It is all a matter of interpretation. Indeed, both opinions could contain a grain of truth, for wisdom and absent-mindedness are not necessarily that far apart. Take that

A splendid model of a tawny owl, made in Copenhagen. In nature, these owls can adapt to the harshest of climates, and thanks to their heightened senses of sight and hearing, they can detect, say, a lemming even when it is hidden under many inches of snow.

ancient Greek philosopher, Thales, who was teased by a
Thracian servant girl for wandering around with his head in
the air, ostensibly to watch the movements of the stars, and
who ended up falling flat on his face in a puddle. The girl
concluded that by looking up into the sky, the sage
neglected to see where he was walking. Philosophers drew a
different moral, namely that Thales only *appeared* absent-
minded and was actually working out complex calculations
that had very practical and profitable implications. In fact,
his calculations led Thales to the conclusion that there
would be a bumper crop of olives that year, and he bought,

*A porcelain owl from Holland. Owls puff up
their feathers into a ball when they want to
frighten a possible enemy, adopting what
animal behaviour experts call the threat
position.*

at low cost, a number of olive presses from unsuspecting
local farmers, who later had to pay through the nose to
repurchase them.

This brings us back to Greece, Pallas Athene, and her
special feathered favourite. The goddess, so the myth relates,
was born out of the head of Zeus, brandishing a lance of
pure gold. As patron of the arts and sciences, deity of
wisdom and victory, and second only to her lord and father
Zeus in the divine hierarchy, warlike Athene (or Minerva,
as she was known to the Romans) symbolized the light of
intelligence and rational thought. She taught humans how
to navigate, weave and spin; how to remain alert, so as to
become wise, shrewd and prudent counsellors; and how to
be successful in battle by fighting with judgement and skill.

The owl became Athene's special creature. Once it had
won her blessing of access to the open spaces of the heavens,
the astute bird gained some benefit from having friends in
high places. Its characteristic hoot was no longer merely an
anonymous, woeful sound but the very embodiment of the
divine word. Athenians, to whose hearts the goddess was so
dear, hailed the bird as her chosen representative and
encouraged it to fly freely about their city, even by day. No
longer reviled for its links with evil deeds and dire spells, the
owl was the epitome of wisdom and prosperity.

By virtue of being Athene's personal emblem, the owl
was, because of its natural habits, a creature of the moon.
The moon, in turn, was the heavenly repository of rational
intelligence and inductive knowledge, as opposed to the
sun, with its blinding light, which was associated with
intuitive brilliance and imagination. The owl was the
creature that could distinguish things from one another,
even in the dark, seeing where others could not see. The
Greek name for owl, *glaux*, also means "gleaming one," a

reference to its big eyes which, like the moon, reflect sunlight.

The ancient Greeks also had a popular saying that conveyed the owl's new-found respectability and popularity. "Taking owls to Athens" was the catch phrase for abundance, rather like "selling refrigerators to Eskimos" or "taking coals to Newcastle." Plenty led to wealth, and so Athenian coins bore the figure of an owl, its name virtually synonymous with money.

On this subject, Plutarch tells a poignant little story in which the owl plays a supporting role. A man named Gylippus had evidently been entrusted with a large sum of public money, and was tempted to steal a sizeable portion of it and hide it under the roof of his house. He was examined by magistrates but made no reply to their searching questions. However, his servant remarked that he had seen a number of owls roosting beneath his master's roof. Since slaves were generally forbidden to accuse their employers, this was a clever, oblique way of reporting the theft without infringing the letter of the law and at the same time doing a great service to the state.

Thanks to the Greeks, therefore, owls were no longer taken to be heralds of disaster. In their preference for solitude and night-time vigils, they came to be compared with sages. Their cry, though still sounding like a lament, was not necessarily a bad omen but rather a salutary warning. Its reputation for sobriety and wisdom was perpetuated. In Rome, the statue of the philosopher-emperor Marcus Aurelius, which stands on the Capitol, was the subject of a medieval legend. On the monument there is a raised part of the mane on the horse that was believed to

A terracotta figure by Pino Sacchi (1987). Following double page: owls from all over the world. From the left: a Mexican papier-mâché owl; two owlets made from dried seed heads and fruits, and a stone owl, all from South America; an Italian owl sitting on a book; a Greek plaster-of-Paris owl; and, behind them, owls made of pottery and porous stone.

be the tuft of feathers of an owl – an owl that at the end of time would restore the statue to its original luster, flying up into the sky to herald, not the usual imminent disaster, but the Last Judgment, the coming of the Kingdom of God.

Even the Christian tradition, despite its apparent aversion to owls and nocturnal creatures in general, has adopted the bird as an emblem of eternity, or at least as a symbol of the

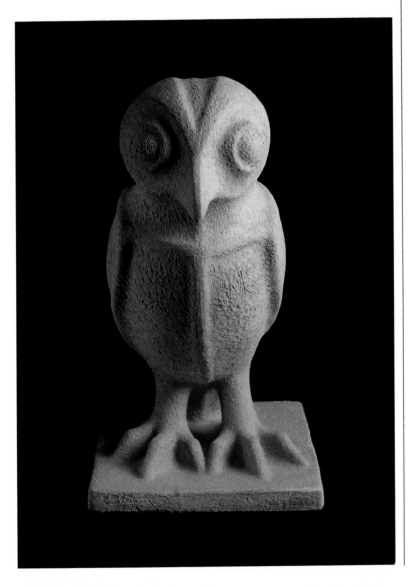

Recent craftwork from Thailand, in lacquered wood. Opposite: a charming little owl covered in coloured beads. This bird certainly has a flirtatious air.

soul's immortality. The Christian symbolism, with allusions to the Crucifixion and the Resurrection, is elaborated by the Italian writer Franco Cardini in an article written on the characteristics of the owl and the more callous forms of treatment meted out during the ages, principally as a consequence of the blindness of unbelievers.

Cardini writes: "The poor owl crucified on the doors of peasant houses . . . thereby vindicates, by means of its martyred corpse, the symbolic heritage of a great many cults and traditions: it is the evil omen that people want to keep at a distance from their homes, but it is also the figure of Divine Wisdom, of the Word that has suffered in the darkness of the Sepulcher before triumphing over it and saving the human race."

For the Greeks, the owl was an embodiment not only of wisdom but also of knowledge and prudence, reflected in its instinctive reaction to retreat gracefully when harried by intruders. It was on the strength of such traits that Antiochus, king of Syria, decided to have his realm's coinage minted with the likeness of an owl above a lion, to indicate that strength was secondary to wisdom.

During the Middle Ages, monks, observing that the owl never moved from its roost the whole day long, regarded it as a symbol for meditation, setting an example for all those who chose to confine themselves in a solitary cell, rejecting the things of this world to become immersed in learned studies and divine mysteries.

In Tibet, too, the owl is compared with the disciple who is serving a period of seclusion, in the course of which the ascetic seeks mastery over his own spirit. The *tsham*, Tibetan word for this solitary phase, may last a few hours or years on end, and is necessarily spent in an isolated room, a corner of

the countryside or even in a cave – surroundings reminiscent of the owl's habitats.

The final word in a chapter that describes the ways in which certain individuals and civilizations have sought to rehabilitate the owl must go to a great French poet, whose beautiful verses reveal him as someone who must have had a genuine understanding of this remarkable bird:

Under black yews that protect them
    The owls perch in a row
Like alien gods whose red eyes
    Glitter. They meditate.

*The delicate balance achieved by the owl in
this metal figurine recalls the movements
adopted by the predator as it watches its
quarry from afar, judging to perfection the
distance and exact position.*

Petrified, they will perch there till
    The melancholy hour
When the slanting sun is ousted,
    And darkness settles down.

From their posture, the wise
    Learn to shun, in this world at least,
Motion and commotion:
    Impassioned by passing shadows,
Man will always be scourged
    For trying to change his place.

(Charles Baudelaire, "Les Hiboux," *Les Fleurs du mal*)

Never closing an eye

Proverbs can usually be found to back up any opinion; and as likely as not, there is another to contradict it. So while many would agree that "Early to bed, early to rise, makes a man healthy, wealthy and wise," some would prefer to base their lives on the precept that "Early to bed, and you'll wish you were dead. Bed before eleven, nuts before seven," or that "Great eaters and great sleepers are incapable of anything else that is great." There may be many good reasons to not waste time sleeping, but what makes somebody become a "night owl"?

People who seldom get a good night's sleep generally come in for sympathy, whether the lack of sleep is due to working the nightshift or purely the result of insomnia. Habitual lack of sleep can affect performance, and to be dead tired most of the time is not exactly conducive to clear thinking and decision making.

There are numerous theories as to the reasons for insomnia. Without delving into deeper causes, it is obvious that sleeplessness, whether occasional or protracted, may be

brought about by worry. People may be over–active
mentally, unhappy in their private or professional lives, or
troubled by conscience or anxiety.

There is no good reason to suppose that owls get less
sleep than other birds, and observation of them in zoos
makes it clear that they spend a good part of the day fast
asleep. Probably we think of them as insomniacs only
because they reverse the natural order of things by carrying
out their normal activities during the night and catching up
on their rest by day. But since they are habitually awake
when sleepless individuals are tossing and turning in their
beds, a link can be found. Once again, however, we must
venture into the realms of legend and superstition in
considering the matter.

If the ancient Romans are to be believed, owls were
constantly tormented by pangs of conscience and it was for
this reason that they passed their nights in keeping terrible
vigil. According to some stories, Julius Caesar, despite the
fact that he had been forewarned by a soothsayer, met his
death by assassination because an owl had appeared in his

bedroom the previous night. The same thing happened to Aurelius Commodus just before he died: an owl perched in his room and cast an evil eye. And a similar fate was evidently reserved for the Emperor Augustus.

Herod Agrippa had the misfortune to fall into disgrace with the Emperor Tiberius, who promptly had him arrested as a result. This happened on the island of Capri, while Agrippa, in all ignorance, was asleep in his villa. The royal centurions took him captive during the night, led him outside and shackled him tightly to a tree. It so happened, however, that an owl was perched on one of the branches,

The twin nature of the owl is nicely caught in the aggressiveness of German Hans Georg's creation below, and in the tenderness of the Hungarian porcelain opposite.

and an unnamed soothsayer who was eyewitness to the incident offered his professional assessment of the situation, predicting that Agrippa would definitely be released and would even become king of Judaea. So far, so good. But the seer qualified his optimistic reading of events by adding that when Agrippa next saw that self-same owl, his life would surely be forfeit. Agrippa doubtless put his trust in the laws of coincidence, looking forward to a long and prosperous life.

Both parts of the soothsayer's prediction were fulfilled. Agrippa was duly enthroned king of Judaea, and his administration was generally approved by the Jews. One night, however, in A.D. 44, as he was enjoying festivities at the amphitheater in Caesarea, on the seacoast of Palestine, he happened to catch sight of that identical owl, despite the time that had elapsed and the considerable distance from the island of Capri. The prophecy came to pass, Agrippa fell ill and within five days he was dead. Fate, the power of suggestion, who knows?

Owls are accused of all kinds of mischief. Our old friend Aelianus, who seems to have had a lively, questing imagination, was convinced that one of their favourite night-time activities was stealing crows' eggs. This supposition may have arisen from the fact that owls occasionally use crows' nests after they have been abandoned for some time (but certainly not when the original occupants still have unhatched eggs inside).

Nevertheless, there are various other traditions that allude to links between these two species, suggesting that they are sworn enemies who regularly indulge in filching each other's eggs, those of the owl vanishing by day and those of the crows at night.

There is a Russian story along the same lines in which the

An owl can be just a cuddly toy, without any frightening overtones, like this one made in softest plush.

A pair of owlets from Hong Kong, based on a Chinese design using the typical tay process. Opposite: another matchbox-label owl, this one from the Soviet Union, dating from the 1960s.

owl, operating by stealth at night, is accused of purloining eggs from the nests of swans and geese.

The antagonistic relationship between owls and crows is mentioned, too, by the Greek philosopher Aristotle in his book *Historia animalium*, which certainly contains many valid observations concerning animal behaviour. It is possible that this mutual hostility, supposing it exists, symbolizes the traditional human conflict between the forces of night and day, between reason, as represented by the owl, and intuition, as exemplified by the crow. It was believed, too, that, if mixed together, owl's blood and crow's blood would never blend, though exactly what kind of recipe was being planned is not revealed.

In the *Panchatantra*, a collection of ancient Indian tales, it is said that the owl, far from being content to steal the crow's eggs, actually launches attacks at night on the nest of the enemy, with the intention of killing it. In this account, owls and crows are permanently engaged in what are literally fights to the death.

This unending war takes on symbolic significance as well. In yet another version of the Parliament of birds, absolute power is entrusted to the owl, but the crow voices its opposition, declaring that its natural foe, the owl, is too cunning to deserve election, and this lone criticism apparently swings the majority decision against the owl.

Before she adopted the owl, Athene was even said to have flaunted the crow as her emblem. The crow, however, blotted its copybook. Apparently the goddess fell in love with a girl who was being pursued by Neptune, god of the

ОХРАНЯЙТЕ ПОЛЕЗНЫХ И РЕДКИХ ПТИЦ И ЗВЕРЕЙ

СОВА-СПЛЮШКА

ГЛАВФАНСПИЧПРОМ Ф-КА «ПРОЛЕТАРСКОЕ ЗНАМЯ» Г.ЧУДОВО ГОСТ 1820-56* 50 ШТ. Ц.1 КОП.1966 г.

sea. In order to protect the girl from Neptune's clutches, Athene turned her into a white crow that accompanied her everywhere. But the ungrateful crow insulted the daughters of Cecrops, king of Attica, who were dear to the goddess. Athene was infuriated by this act of rudeness, sent the scandal monger packing with a black mark on its plumage and chose the owl as her new favourite.

Already worshipped as the deity of tempests and thunderbolts, Athene was subsequently recognized as the wise warrior goddess as well. From then on, she was always portrayed with an owl's head or wearing a helmet bearing the likeness of an owl.

Not all other birds automatically shun the owl, and there are apparently various examples of cooperation. Pliny, for example, mentions that the sparrowhawk often benefits from such an association, and in return will come to the aid of the owl if the latter is attacked.

Gené, writing much later, suggests that owls and doves are sufficiently trusting of each other to roost together in dovecotes. Furthermore, if owls happen to be observed in such a situation, this is more likely to be a sign of impending good fortune than of ill-omen. The ancient Franks strictly prohibited the killing of any owl that took shelter in a dovecote.

The owl's habit of staying awake at night has also been explained as avarice, for it is so attached to its possessions that it stands guard over them to repel intruders. It is anyone's guess as to who these potential thieves might be and what valuables might tempt them. The sensible explanation, of course, is that the owl's constant vigilance is a necessary element of its hunting operations and feeding requirements. But far-fetched theories such as the former ones are undeniably more fun.

This curious item is a water dispenser in porous earthenware. The water contained inside the owl gradually seeps into the flower pot. Here the owl seems to be playing the kind of fertility role it gained from its association with the goddess Athene.

Artemidorus, the Greek author of the *Onirocriticon* (a treatise on dreams that may have been one of the source references of Sigmund Freud), maintains that because owls are sluggish and indolent by day, they get up to all kinds of mischief at night. Dreaming about them, therefore, is an unhealthy sign, for it warns of imminent contact with undesirable people who do their work mainly at night.

Such social outcasts might include thieves, smugglers (in Britain owls and smugglers are often linked in popular lore) or any kind of villainous person planning subterfuge action against you. Dreams of this nature should thus be taken as a warning to keep on the alert. However, Artemidorus also thought that these future relationships with those who work at night could include guardians and protectors. In this light, it is interesting to note that in Italy, in the city of Bologna, a policeman on the beat is sometimes known as a *gufo*, owl,

Modern owl-pattern lacework from Bruges.
Opposite: an attractive stylized owl made of
clay by a young craftsman from Puglia,
Italy. The bird's perch is actually a whistle.

and that throughout the country the word *civetta*, small owl, is used to describe a police patrol car.

Dreams, nevertheless, are not necessarily negative and ominous. Some interpreters declare that eyes represent an open mind; and because owls' eyes are so large and prominent, it stands to reason that dreams about the bird point to our being in a state of vigilance (albeit subconscious) concerning a problem of single importance that our conscious mind may be underestimating or ignoring. Because the owl "knows the darkness of the subconscious," this, then, is a positive dream that may not

only help to indicate how best we may resolve that particular problem but may even herald considerable changes in our personality.

The fact that the owl is a symbol of vigilance is attested by classical iconography. Moreover, vigilance is in some respects a form of protection, and the owl will perform this function if requested to do so. To the Tartars, owls were sacred birds, and one famous story tells how their emperor, Genghis Khan, was saved from certain death by the providential intervention of an owl.

The warrior khan had on this occasion been defeated by the enemy and was fleeing the battlefield with a small band of trusty followers. At one point he found shelter under a tree; and on a branch of this tree was perched an owl. His pursuers caught up with him but did not pause to investigate, because they did not believe that anyone could be so foolish as to hide beneath a tree on which such an unlucky bird was sitting. On they rode to continue their search elsewhere, and in this way Genghis Khan was saved.

Hunters may reap advantage from the proverbial vigilance of the owl. In the New World, opossum hunters used to count on the owl to provide them with valuable information. Three hoots from the left were supposed to mean that there were no opposums in the woods near by, whereas three hoots from the right signified that the animals were lurking not far away.

An American fable describes how one unfortunate hunter, whose catch bags remained empty, was so overcome with hunger that he started wandering deliberately into the wilderness to die. On the way, he met a stranger with a large hooked nose who questioned him as to the reason for his desperate state. After listening

Below: an owl made from a variety of materials; the base is terracotta, the rest pitch, bits of glass, beads and plenty of paint. Opposite: a valuable painted silk fan from the mid nineteenth century.

sympathetically to the hunter's sad tale, the mysterious traveller calmed him with the assurance that he would find the answer to all his trials the very next day. With that, the stranger vanished, and in his place stood a large owl. The following day saw a miraculous reversal of the hunter's fortunes.

This story implies that the owl's intervention was somehow associated with magical powers and, indeed, as already noted, the raptor's links with witchcraft are widely believed. Frazer, in *The Golden Bough*, relates that in West Africa, the witch doctors are required, during the "blood-brotherhood" initiation, to mingle their own blood with that of an animal. And whereas the blood bond is likely to be established with one of the more ferocious species, such as a leopard, snake or crocodile, night birds such as the owl are an acceptable alternative.

Witches proper are renowned, of course, for preparing a variety of brews and potions as the crucial ingredients of their spells and the very basis of their magic. In the next chapter, therefore, we shall be looking more deeply at witches' cauldrons and the part that owls play in these black arts.

A proud figure of an owl made in eighteenth-century China. The piece is in precious rock crystal that has been ground by hand. Also from the Far East is the legend that an owl perched on a branch saved the future Emperor Genghis Khan from certain death. At least, that is the Tartars' story.

Sorcerers' apprentices

Tireless and ever watchful, the owl was an ideal companion for that dabbler in magic potions and spells, the wizard. It is unlikely that many ever clapped eyes on such a pair of conspirators. Nevertheless, superstitious ways were such that all you needed was a built-in prejudice against anyone who behaved in an unusually eccentric manner, preferably with sinister features and unsocial habits, a succession of unexplained disasters (epidemics were particularly appropriate), a vivid imagination and a talent for gossip.

Visualize, then the wizard in his peaked hat and flowing robe adorned with mysterious symbols, magic wand in hand, spell book at his side, muttering imprecations and mixing devilish brews. And there, perched high on top of the bookcase is his ally and guardian, the wise old owl, unruffled witness to the preparation of innumerable concoctions intended, for better or worse, to alter the course of human destinies.

A powerful wizard, acknowledged as master of his art, would set special value on his feathered colleague. For the

Another matchbox label featuring an owl, this one from Belgium. Opposite: an enamel vase with an all-round decoration of owls and flowers, made in Hong Kong.

owl, with its extraordinary powers of observation and ability to memorize complicated formulas, would come to be regarded as a veritable encyclopedia of spells. The wizard, after all, was reputed to suffer from absent-mindedness, whereas nothing could possibly escape the ever-vigilant bird of the night.

Worth its weight in gold, the owl might nevertheless be compelled now and then to defend itself against unscrupulous traps and conspiracies by less gifted and less successful magicians seeking to discover its secrets and thus enhance their own reputations, even resorting to kidnapping. History does not record whether such underhand methods succeeded, but it is unlikely. For everyone knows that the owl is basically loyal by nature. Once it has found its wizard, it will stick by him through thick and thin.

Take, for instance, the owl that served Merlin in Arthurian romance. The bird frequently witnessed its master committing appalling errors that sometimes involved them both in dire difficulties. Yet though it might have expressed disapproval and irritation, it never took drastic action. It might well grumble, huff and puff dramatically, face the wall and cover its eyes to spare itself further embarrassment. It might even, in extreme cases, fly off for a while. But it always came back soon to check whether the mistake had been rectified, and if not, to put things right on its own.

This loyalty on the part of apprentice owls, however, is not invariably repaid in equal measure by their masters. Far from trusting his apprentice, let alone sharing his knowledge, the sorcerer generally assumes sole

responsibility for the successful outcome of his experiments, and treats the owl on the bookcase with little more than toleration. If anything happens to go wrong, as likely as not it will be the unfortunate bird that has to take the blame as well as the brunt of its master's wrath. Unless it ducks the deluge of spell books that are hurled in its direction, it risks injury or, worse still, may end up as a deluxe ingredient for the evil-looking soup bubbling in the pot.

As is all too common in the animal world, especially when humans are around, the bird may, in fact, turn out to be of more value dead than alive. Even the most

*A faithful reproduction of a small Attic vase
created in Olympia in 500 B.C. Following
double page: an owl made of wood with eyes
of blown glass by Gualtiero Michelangeli
from Orvieto, Italy.*

inexperienced wizard or witch knows the remarkable
magical properties of owl soup, a fundamental brew to
accompany the most powerful spells. Ovid, for example,
lists all the ingredients of the magic potion prepared by the
sorceress Medea for Aeson, father of her lover Jason:
particularly significant additions to this recipe are a pair of
owl's wings, apparently included with a view to improving
the old man's eyesight. By drinking the concoction Aeson is
guaranteed to recover his youth; and apparently it works.

In Shakespeare's *Macbeth*, too, the evil hags on the blasted
heath recommend, among other ingredients, "lizard's leg"
and "owlet's wing." Their spells evidently work and their
predictions of Macbeth's rise to royal power and eventual
downfall and death come true.

For Shakespeare, the owl was clearly a bird of ill-omen.
In the same play, images of the owl are repeatedly evoked as
Macbeth and his wife go about their bloody business of
killing King Duncan as he sleeps. At the moment her
husband enters Duncan's chamber, knife in hand, she speaks
of "... the owl that shrieked, the fatal bellman, Which gives
the stern'st good-night ..." As he emerges, the deed done,
and asks whether she heard a noise, she replies, "I heard the
owl scream and the crickets cry ..."

In a more mundane context, there are traditional
Yorkshire sayings to the effect that a nice owl soup,
presumably in moderate doses, is an excellent remedy for
whooping cough. In this day and age of animal protection,
the genuine recipe may, in any event, be hard to come by;
but the authentic version is said to beat any modern
medicine.

In the absence of a live owl, substitutes are sometimes
acceptable. Owls' eggs, for example, may be utilized in
potions as a cure for a wide range of ailments and are
indispensable to the well-stocked medicine cupboard.

Owl's egg soup is reckoned to be effective against epilepsy, the only snag being that it has to be prepared when the moon is on the wane. An egg applied to the head in the form of a poultice is accounted a wonderful treatment for thin hair roots – a practice mentioned by Pliny, although he expresses some scepticism.

Pliny does, however, enthusiastically recommend owl's eggs as an effective cure for various kinds of excessive indulgences, notably that of heavy drinking, maintaining that even one egg is sufficient to clear the head. Philostratus, too, argues that the same dose of a single egg is capable of

A brightly-coloured ash tray in enamelled metal from Thailand. Opposite: a recently made hand-chased silver pot from Florence. Two very different ways of using our friend the owl as receptacle.

producing a total aversion to wine even in someone who has never drunk any before. Similar prescriptions claim that owl's eggs cooked in wine for three days will cure the worst cases of drunkenness. And since it is never too early to start, catch the patient young. Give an owl's egg to a child and he or she will display a lasting revulsion to wine and lead a life of complete temperance.

This reputation did not go down too well in some divine circles. Dionysus, the god of wine, was, for obvious reasons, intensely hostile to the bird, as is illustrated in the story of Alcithoe, Leucippe and Arsippe. These three young and hard-working sisters refused even to take time off to attend the celebrations in honour of Dionysus, preferring to stay at home to concentrate on their weaving and embroidery (activities, incidentally, that were approved by the goddess Athene). It has to be said, in fairness, that in the course of such festivities, drinking was apt to lead to more dissolute activities, so the three Greek sisters were obviously aware of the risks they would be running.

Be that as it may, the god was so offended that they did not come to honour him in the customary manner that he swooped down on the girls like one of the Furies and turned them then and there into the creatures he most loathed –

owls. Their weaving looms and embroidery frames miraculously sprouted vine shoots and leaves, and enormous bunches of succulent grapes, whereupon the terrified owls flew away.

So well established was the association of the owl with sobriety that in classical iconography the bird is often chosen to symbolize absolute abstention from drink.

Ancient medicine, too, lists a number of prescriptions for sweetening the breath of immoderate drinkers, and all of them include owl's eggs as a fundamental ingredient. This consensus is evidently based on the traditional precepts of sympathetic medicine, whereby eating an animal or parts of it enables the patient not only to benefit from the meat itself but also to absorb the physical and moral characteristics of that creature – cunning, strength, wisdom and the like. In this particular context, then, the implication is that since wine confers on the drinker a temporary madness that produces impenetrable fumes and clouds the reason, clear-sightedness can only be restored by consuming a product of a bird known for its acute vision.

In this ancient art of sympathetic medicine, it is logical that the exceptional eyesight of the owl would take on special significance. The really ideal way of acquiring perfect vision is to eat the owl's eyes; but since this may not commend itself to everyone, and in view of the difficulties involved in procuring these organs, the eggs are acknowledged to have a similar effect.

Pursuing this line of argument, since a good pair of eyes can penetrate the veil of falsehood and reach the truth, it stands to reason that should we suspect a person of being a persistent liar, the best solution is to go out and catch a compliant owl. The rest is plain sailing. Simply remove the bird's heart and right claw and place these items on the chest

This modern small bottle in blown glass, made to resemble an owl, is really a table cruet for oil and vinegar. Historically, owls are more used to providing wizards and witches with a variety of very different ingredients.

of the culprit while asleep. In answer to a pointed question, he or she will then give a true account of what has actually occurred or been perpetrated.

Once a full confession has been obtained, and appropriate action taken, be sure not to throw away these magical parts for they can be used again for a completely different purpose. Evidently, being followed around by dogs was a commonplace hazard of everyday life because you just had to tuck those bits and pieces under your armpits in order to keep the animals away.

Be careful, however, not to get your instructions confused. There is an Indian belief, for example, that the meat of an owl is a potent aphrodisiac. On the other hand, in other places and at other times, this tasty morsel could cause loss of memory and, if you are particularly unfortunate, result in complete insanity.

Below: a plastic feeding bottle in the shape of an owl, from the United States. The trademark reads, "made in Ravenna, Ohio, Evenflo Co." Opposite: a "Tea for Two" with stacking cups, an example of pure English kitsch.

Better perhaps not to meddle with such potentially dangerous experiments and heed the wisdom of that aspect of folk medicine that recommends placing some owl feathers under your pillow in order to get a decent night's sleep, and advocates straining your ears to hear the magical hooting of an owl, guaranteed to banish the severest symptoms of influenza.

It comes as no surprise to learn that the owl can have such a variety of beneficial effects on even chronic ailments when you consider that this bird was not only the sacred emblem of Athene but also of Asclepius, son of Apollo and the nymph Coronis, god of medicine. And after all, medicine is, in many primitive and ancient societies, merely an extension and complement of magic, as the figure of the witch doctor readily attests. So there is no real contradiction

Group photograph of a family of barn-owls made of marble dust and plaster-of-Paris by an Italian craftsman in the 1960s. Barn-owls, in fact, do raise big families.

in believing the owl to be both the sorcerer's apprentice and the healer's companion.

Given that dual role, it is understandable that the owl is seen variously as both a power of good and of evil. In mythology, moreover, its negative and positive aspects merge and offset each other, without apparent conflict. Neither of them, taken alone, assumes overriding significance.

The fact remains, however, that it is much easier sometimes to see things in terms of extremes, white or black, good or bad. And where owls are concerned, majority opinion would seem to come down in favour of black. Superstition, which can still exploit owls to avert the evil eye, will always survive in a rational world: in the world of the imagination, there is respect and sympathy, and superstition has no place there.

Unfortunately, realism, logic, pragmatism, call it what you will, all too often has no patience with myths, fairy tales and the like. Reason looks askance at imagination. But our lives, if they are to be fruitful, even at times endurable, must necessarily include a fair proportion of both, inextricably mingled. And no matter how foolish or fanciful some of the notions may seem (instant cures for drunkenness, stomach ache or whatever), we could perhaps indulge ourselves to the extent of showing a measure of gratitude and respect for this bird, which is reputedly able to utter the divine word and penetrate to the heart of all mysteries.

If, despite this, we continue to display cruelty and ingratitude, the owl would be best advised never to abandon the world of the imagination for that of reality, and to stay put in a tranquil place where to die is to be born again and where nobody ever ends up nailed to the door of a house.

Hunting for owls

We could go hunting for owls in amongst trees, rocks and barns, but it is also possible to find them in rather more tranquil surroundings. Since our friends are inveterate lovers of peace and silence, what better place to look for them than in a bookshop or library? We have already seen that owls are quite at home among books, perching undisturbed on top of a shelf or gliding around among dusty volumes of fables, myths and fairy tales. So let us open the pages and select a few passages by well-known authors that celebrate their distinctive virtues.

An owl-shaped eighteenth-century English copper ink stand. The head lifts up so that the pen can be dipped into the ink. This object is very much in keeping with the proverbial wisdom of the owl and its alleged passion for books, libraries and quiet places of study.

Owls often feature in children's picture books, comic stories and cartoon films in all sorts of appealing roles. This friendly owl from a children's picture book is in the story of "Bambi."

FELIX SALTEN, **Bambi**

The young fawn, who owes much of his popularity to the successful cartoon film of Walt Disney, begins to take his first steps in the forest and to get to know the creatures who live there; among them, of course, are the owls.

At night the woods were solemn and still. There were only a few voices. They sounded loud in the stillness, and they had a different ring from daytime voices, and left a deeper impression.

Bambi liked to see the owl. She had such a wonderful flight, perfectly light and perfectly noiseless. She made as little sound as a butterfly, and yet she was dreadfully big. She had such striking features, too, so pronounced and so deeply thoughtful. And such wonderful eyes! Bambi admired her firm, quietly courageous glance. He liked to listen when she talked to his mother or to anyone else. He would stand a little to one side, for he was somewhat afraid of the masterful glance that he admired so much. He did not understand most of the clever things she said, but he knew they were clever, and they pleased him and filled him with respect for the owl.

Then the owl would begin to hoot. "Hooah! – Ha! – Ha! – Haaa-ah!" she would cry. It sounded different from the thrushes' song, or the yellow-birds', different from the friendly notes of the cuckoo, but Bambi loved the owl's cry, for he felt its mysterious earnestness, its unutterable wisdom and strange melancholy.

Then there was the screech-owl, a charming little fellow, lively and gay with no end to his inquisitiveness. He was bent on attracting attention. "Oi! yeek! oi! yeek!" he would call in a terrible high-pitched piercing voice. It sounded as if he were on the point of death. But he was really in a beaming good humour and was hilariously happy whenever he frightened somebody. "Oi! yeek!" he would cry so dreadfully loud that the forests heard it for a mile around. But afterwards he would laugh with a soft chuckle, though you could only hear it if you stood close by.

Bambi discovered that the screech-owl was delighted whenever he frightened anyone, or when anybody thought that something dreadful had happened to him. After that, whenever Bambi met him, he never failed to rush up and ask, "What has happened to you?" or to say with a sigh, "O, how you frightened me just now!" Then the owl would be delighted.

"O yes," he would say, laughing, "it sounds pretty gruesome." He would puff up his feathers into a greyish-white ball and look extremely handsome.

EDWARD LEAR, **The Owl and the Pussy Cat and other nonsense** and **There was an old man from Dumbree**

This well-known nonsense rhyme tells the tale of an owl's love for a cat. The romance of the two animals adrift at sea is so convincing that no other love story seemed more likely than this "nonsense song."

The Owl and the Pussy-cat went to sea
  In a beautiful pea-green boat,
They took some honey, and plenty of
  money,
    Wrapped up in a five-pound note.
The Owl looked up to the stars above,

And sang to a small guitar,
"O lovely Pussy! O Pussy, my love,
  What a beautiful Pussy you are,
    You are,
    You are!
What a beautiful Pussy you are!"

Limericks are Irish nonsense poems that originated from the town of Limerick on the estuary of the river Shannon. They consist of five lines, the first nearly always ending in the name of the place where the poem's action occurs, and the last taking up the idea of the opening line. In the entertaining world of these rhymes, extraordinary and curious things happen, as in Edward Lear's limerick about a man from Dumbree, a Scottish-sounding place that is not in any atlas.

There was an old man of Dumbree
Who taught little owls to drink tea.
For he said, "To eat mice
Is not proper or nice",
That amiable old man of Dumbree.

GRIMM, **Household Tales**

The Parliament of Birds is assembled in order to decide what punishment should be meted out to the wren, who has used deception to win the contest and so make fools of the other birds. The owl has the task of keeping guard over the prisoner, who has been shut in a hole. But, as we saw earlier, the owl did not fulfil his commitment. . .

The owl was placed as sentinel in front of it, and was not to let the rascal out if she had any value for her life. When evening was come, all the birds were feeling very tired after exerting their wings so much, so they went to bed with their wives and children. The owl alone remained standing by the mouse-hole, gazing steadfastly into it with her great eyes. In the meantime she, too, had grown tired and thought to herself, "You might certainly shut one eye, you will still watch with the other, and the little miscreant shall not come out of his hole." So she shut one eye, and with the other looked straight at the mouse-hole. The little fellow put his head out and peeped, and wanted to slip away, but the owl came forward immediately, and he drew his head back again. Then the owl opened the one eye again, and shut the other, intending to shut them in turn all through the night.

But when she next shut the one eye, she forgot to open the other, and as soon as

Depicted as a philosopher, complete with pipe to help him concentrate, this owl, from a cartoon, is one of many "wise old owls" in children's stories.

both her eyes were shut she fell asleep. The little fellow soon observed that, and slipped away.

From that day forth, the owl has never dared to show herself by daylight, for if she does, the other birds chase her and pluck her feathers out. She only flies out by night, but hates and pursues mice because they make such ugly holes.

COLETTE, **The Tawny Owls**

Who better than Colette to tell us about these mysterious and vilified hunters of the night?

In the dark days they come into their own. When the trees are muffled in motionless, dripping mist, they perch there and sing. Hoot-owls and sparrow-owls, screech-owls and eagle-owls, they exchange quavering laughs, sobs, soft whistlings and those poignant cries that only the night ever hears. In the half-light the little sparrow-owl shows his charming cat face, his colour blending with that of the oak leaves; the eagle-owl leaves his tower before the accustomed time and hovers for a moment, huge and russet-red as a sparrow-hawk; but the swiftly falling night releases and hides the entire patrol. Invisible though they now are, one can guess, from the light, mocking laughter and faint, persistent calls, how many of them there are on the watch around these old walls. But their wings brush against nothing, their feathers make no rustling sound, and their ghostly flight avoids alike the branch, the wall, and the bars of the gable window.

When the rim of the black sky lifts to reveal the dark red of a winter dawn, quickly blotted out by the mist, the owls come back home. One of them – is it always the same one? – utters, as though to warn me, the heart-rending cry of a cock in the night, a clarion call that sounds like an ironical command: "Wake up, all of you, I'm going to sleep!" I obey and sometimes lean out of my window to watch the return of the tawny owls.

Below me are fifty feet of mist, a shade whiter than the night above, or the oak trees rustling faintly like dry palm leaves under the rising wind. Fifty feet of mist, full of the muffled flight of swift creatures weaving to and fro like the effortless circling of fish in the sea. My eyes grow accustomed and the sky pales. Little by little I can distinguish the colours – russet-red and white, yellow and grey – on the great wings widespread and planing below me, and on the speckled backs and fan-like tails.

An illustration from another children's book, in which a gallant owl leaves an attractive rabbit in no doubt of his feelings for her.

A wing passes so close to me that it wafts against my temples the delicate damp of the morning and the odour of withered leaves.

They quicken their pace, circling and rising. The snow-blue sky is streaked with silent birds. A narrow opening under the ledge of a pointed turret roof swallows them one by one as they pass. At the hour when the sheep-dogs begin to bark, invisible far below under the mist, only a snowy-owl remains, a "white lady" sitting on the sill of a loft. Blinking her eyelids she puffs herself up, coquettishly fluffing out the narrow brown piping which holds her little Mary Stuart bonnet closely round her shapely cheeks.

FLORIAN, **The Philosopher and the Screech-Owl**

Owls often figure in the fables of Jean-Pierre Claris de Florian, who wrote in the late eighteenth century. The main character in this one is an old screech-owl, closely related to ordinary owls but no better treated than they are.

Persecuted and proclaimed,
Chased from his retreat, diffamed,
For no other reason save
Their own names to things he gave,
Lived a poor philosopher,
From town to town a wanderer,
Carrying with him, as his pack,
Reason – all else did he lack.
One day, while in meditation
On his last night's lucubration,
In a spacious forest side
Lo! a screech-owl he espied;
Jays and jackdaws roundabout
Harassed him and shouted out:
"Rogue, by earth and heaven banned!
Traitor to his native land!
We must pluck him all alive;
Yes, yes, pluck him, pluck belive;
After we will sound his knell."
Straight they rushed on him pell-mell:
He, poor creature! ill bestead,
Turned, re-turned, his fine large head;
Told him reasons – 'twas no boot –
Excellent beyond dispute.
Touched with sorrow for his bane,
(For philosophy makes men
More soft-hearted and humane),
This our sage soon caused to fly
All that hostile company;
Then to the owl inquiringly:
"What made those assassins seek
On your life their wrath to wreak?
What hast done?" – "No harm have I
Done them," was the owl's reply:
"All my crime is, I have sight
To see clearly in the night."

An entertaining owl study by Emilio
Tadini. Acrylic on canvas, 1978.

Household words the world over
Brief glossary of owls in four languages

English

owl *n.*, *dim.* owlet; *adj.* owlish; a nocturnal bird of prey, well known for its
melancholy "hoot" || (*fig.*) applied to a
person of nocturnal habits, given to
staying out at night || *wise old owl*, per-
son with an appearance of gravity or
wisdom || *screech-owl decoy*, lure, trick
used to entice someone into a trap || *owl
train*, train operating at night.
owl *vb.*, to behave like an owl, to pry
about, prowl, esp. in the dark (*now
mainly pop.*).
owl-light *n.*, the dim light in which
owls roam abroad; twilight, dusk.
night owl *n.*, person who stays up late
at night.

French

hibou *n.m.*, (pl. hiboux) owl || (*fig.*)

misanthrope: *air, aspect, mine de hibou*,
sad, melancholy expression || *des yeux
de hibou*, round, staring eyes || *un nid,
une retraite de hiboux*, an old, uninhabi-
ted house || *être un vrai hibou*, shun so-
ciety, remain an outsider || *faire le hibou*,
stay away from others, keep silent ||
demeurer, vivre en hibou, live solitary.
chouette *n.f.*, owl || (*fig.*) *vieille
chouette*, annoying old woman || *des
yeux de chouette*, large, round eyes || *faire
la chouette*, play alone against a number
of people at billiards, etc. || *être la
chouette de . . .*, hold one's own against
others || *jeu de la chouette*, game similar
to snakes and ladders || *il fait la chouette à
trois personnes*, he is in correspondence
with three people || *il est leur chouette*, he
is the target for their jokes || *adj.* (*pop.
fam.*) *elle est chouette*, said of a woman
who is pleasant company, whose behaviour is praiseworthy, or of a thing

109

that is beautiful, perfect of its kind ‖ *c'est chouette*, very nice, worthwhile ‖ *chouette alors!*, exclamation of satisfaction and pleasure.

Italian

gufo *v. m.*, owl. (*fig.*) a person who is gloomy, anti-social ‖ *fare il gufo* or *fare la vita del gufo*, to lead a retired, solitary life ‖ *avere del gufo*, to be misanthropic ‖ have a myopic, uncertain attitude, not welcoming the light of truth and knowledge ‖ an ugly, graceless individual ‖ object of derision, said of person who is easily duped ‖ *fare il gufo*, to act like a bird of ill-omen, bearing bad news ‖ (*marit.*) apparatus for interfering with enemy radar.

guffagine *n.f.*, misanthropy.

gufare *v. i.*, to call like an owl ‖ (*by exten.*) to give out noisy or hostile signs of indifference ‖ to dupe, to deride; to announce bad tidings ‖ to hide, to conceal oneself, to pull covers over head.

guffeggiare *v. i.*, to move about awkwardly.

gufesco *adj.*, asocial, gloomy, irritable.

civetta *n.f.*, owl. (*fig.*) *far la civetta* or *esser civetta*, said of a woman who enjoys attracting and flirting with men or of a man who is fickle, moody ‖ *civetta spennata*, an elderly, coquettish woman ‖ *occhi di civetta*, yellowish eyes; (*pop.*) gold pieces ‖ *naso a* or *di civetta*, pointed, curved nose ‖ *far civetta*, to duck the head quickly to avoid a blow; to bow or grovel ‖ *mangiare come le civette*, to eat rapidly and untidily, without chewing ‖ *anche le civette impaniano*, even thieves let themselves be caught ‖ *schiacciare il capo alla civetta*, to give up a big gain for a smaller advantage ‖ *tirare alla civetta*, to take revenge on an innocent person ‖ *cercar uova di civetta*, to embark on a hopeless enterprise ‖ *far come le civette: tutto mio tutto mio*, said of someone who takes everything for himself, including what does not belong to him ‖ *nave civetta*, camouflaged merchant ship, used during First World War in submarine warfare ‖ *auto civetta*, police car used for special

This owl on a matchbox label comes from Italy, but it is obviously destined for an Anglo-Saxon market, where the widsom of the owl has a strong tradition.

German

Eule *n.f.*, owl || *Eulen nach Athen tragen*, take owls to Athens, carry coals to Newcastle || (*marit.*) *eine Eule fangen* to have a headwind || *klug wie eine Eule sein*, to be as cunning as an owl || (*prov.*) *des einen Eule ist anderen Nachtigall*, one man's meat is another man's poison || *ein Gesicht machen wie eine Eule am Mittag*, to look very tired.

Kauz *n.m.*, owl || (*fig.*) (*Sonderling*) original, eccentric person || *ein komischer Krauz*, an odd fellow || *lustiger Kauz*, a happy companion || *närrischer Kauz*, a clown, bright spark || (*pop.*) chignon, bun || *das Haar zu einem Kauz aufstecken*, make a chignon, put hair in a bun.

Käuschen *n. n.*, little owl || *ein niedliches Käuzche*, a teasing flirt.

operations || summary of a daily paper or magazine, attached to news stands to attract attention of passers-by || *notizia civetta*, information published to sound out public opinion.

civettare *v. i.*, (*fig.*) to play the coquette, to attract or flatter someone.

civetteria *n.f.*, habit of flirting; feminine behaviour designed to attract a man || spontaneous, delightful movement or behaviour, as of a baby or child || (*by exten.*) insistence on drawing attention to oneself or to one's actions.

civettio *n.m.*, feminine chatter or activity designed to attract men, or simply to show off.

civettonne *n.m.*, an elderly Don Juan.

civettuolo *adj.*, spontaneously charming, attractive or provocative (in positive sense) || smiling, catching the eye by its appearance or novelty.

Opposite: a work by Mauro Staccioli entitled "Spite" (1987). Various materials have been used here, including a fine alabaster owl by Mino Scarselli.

Acknowledgements

The authors would like to thank the owl enthusiasts who contributed so much with their collections. Special thanks go to: Franco Fossati, Piero Piani, Sergio Abbiati, Paolo Galeotti, Carlo Violani, Erminio Caprotti, Alberto Mari, Patrizia Maione, Monica Castiglioni and in particular to Emma Ghisotti for her invaluable help.

The publisher thanks Gruppo Mantero for allowing the reproduction of the Interseta design on the cover.

Picture sources

The owls illustrated in this volume belong to the following collections:
Wolfgang Hilinger, Milan (pp. 4, 10, 11, 12, 14, 15, 22, 24, 27, 28, 29, 35, 38, 42, 46, 51, 53, 55, 56, 58, 60, 66, 67, 68, 71, 72, 73, 76, 80, 83, 84, 87, 89, 94, 95, 98, 100);
Margherita Bottini, Milan (pp. 7, 8–9, 23, 30, 32–33, 40, 48–49, 57, 82, 90, 96, 99, 102);
Prof. Rossana Bossaglia (pp. 17, 19, 21, 34, 37, 39, 44, 45, 54, 63, 74, 79, 81, 110);
Adriana Giussani, Milan (pp. 64–65, 92–93, cover);
Matteo Guarnaccia (pp. 50, 77, 88, 111);

All photographs by Giorgio Coppin in collaboration with Anna Giorgetti.

Illustrations

p. 75	Cuddly toy: by Italian toy manufacturer Trudi
p. 104	Illustration taken from: *Le grandi favole a fumetti*, published in Italy by Arnoldo Mondadori Editore S.p.A.
p.106	Illustration taken from: *Le nostre prime leggendarie imprese*, published in Italy by Arnoldo Mondadori Editore S.p.A.
p. 107	Illustration taken from: *Le prime rime di Susanna* by Colette Rosselli, published in Italy by Arnoldo Mondadori Editore S.p.A.